101 Ways to Lull Your Baby to Sleep

CIDER MILL PRESS ★ KENNEBUNKPORT, ME

13-Digit ISBN: 9781604336733
10-Digit ISBN: 1604336730

This book may be ordered by mail from the publisher. Please include $5.95 for postage and handling. Please support your local bookseller first!

Books published by Cider Mill Press Book Publishers are available at special discounts for bulk purchases in the United States by corporations, institutions, and other organizations. For more information, please contact the publisher.

Cider Mill Press Book Publishers
"Where good books are ready for press"
PO Box 454, 12 Spring Street
Kennebunkport, Maine 04046

Visit us on the Web! www.cidermillpress.com

Design by Sara Corbett

All images are used under official license from Shutterstock.com

Text Permissions:
Text on page 29 is from The No-Cry Sleep Solution by Elizabeth Pantley, copyright © 2002 by Elizabeth Pantley. Reprinted with permission from McGraw-Hill Education.

Text on page 56 is reprinted with the permission of Scribner, a division of Simon & Schuster, Inc. from YOU: Raising Your Child: The Owner's Manual from First Breath to First Grade by Michael F. Roizen, MD and Mehmet C. Oz, MD. Copyright © 2010 by Michael F Roizen and Oz Works LLC. All rights reserved.

Text on pages 80–81 is reprinted with the permission of Fireside, a division of Simon & Schuster, Inc. from Solve Your Child's Sleep Problems, New, Expanded and Revised by Richard Ferber, M.D. Copyright © 1985, 2006 by Richard Ferber, M.D. All rights reserved.

Text on pages 120–121 is from Sleeping Through The Night, Revised Edition by Jodi A. Mindell, Ph.D. Copyright © 2005 by Jodi A. Mindell. Reprinted by permission of HarperCollins Publishers.

Text on page 131 is from The Baby Sleep Solution: A Proven Program To Teach Your Baby To Sleep For Twelve Hours A Night by Suzy Giordano, with Lisa Abidin, copyright © 2006 by Suzy Giordano and Lisa Abidin. Used by permission of Dutton, an imprint of Penguin Publishing Group, a division of Penguin Random House LLC.

All other credited excerpts are used with permission by the credited author.

Printed in China

1 2 3 4 5 6 7 8 9 0

First Edition

101 Ways to Lull Your Baby to Sleep

BY **ALEXANDRA PAIGE**

WITH A FOREWORD BY RONI COHEN LEIDERMAN, PH.D

CIDER MILL PRESS ★ KENNEBUNKPORT, ME

A NOTE ABOUT SAFETY

Always use your best judgment when implementing any of the ideas and methods suggested in this book, and keep in mind that the safest sleep position for a baby is on his back, on a firm surface. The American Academy of Pediatrics' official policy statement, titled "SIDS and Other Sleep-Related Infant Deaths: Expansion of Recommendations for a Safe Infant Sleeping Environment," published in 2011, states: "To reduce the risk of SIDS, infants should be placed for sleep in a supine position (wholly on the back) for every sleep by every caregiver until 1 year of life." The policy also strictly warns against bed-sharing with your baby, using soft or cushy mattresses and bedding, covering your baby's head while he sleeps (with a hat or blanket), or allowing soft toys or loose bedding in your baby's crib. So, keep in mind that even if your baby falls asleep in a swing, on a couch, or in a car seat, you should always transfer your snoozing little one to his crib and ensure he's safely on his back once he's down for the count.

(To learn more, read the full policy statement at www.aap.org.)

CONTENTS

Getting your little one to sleep isn't always the easiest task, but it may be the one that—years from now—you'll look back and miss the most. Rocking a restless baby until she's peacefully asleep and heavy in your arms is one of the quiet joys of parenthood. We've brainstormed more than 101 ways to lull your little one to sleep, whether you're in need of a foolproof sleep routine to implement from here on out, or a quick fix on an especially challenging evening. From pediatricians and "Mommy Bloggers" to new moms and dads to doting grandparents, we asked dozens of experts in the field to tell us about their most successful—and most innovative—paths to sleep success.

In this book, you'll find ideas in the form of anecdotes, straightforward advice, and even lists of apps and devices that can help soothe a fussy baby. The ideas range from classic standbys (*how to choose the right bedtime story*) to quirky suggestions (*dance with baby!*), but each comes highly recommended by someone who's struggled with a sleepless baby. Our ideas are geared toward a broad range of temperaments and sleep situations, and while some are perfect for newborns, others may be more fitting for an older baby. So, take each suggestion with a grain of salt. No one knows your baby, your home environment, or your own preferred routine like you do, so use your judgment—only *you* can truly know which sleep solutions are a good fit for your baby, and which just aren't. And if you're ever in doubt about the proper way to incorporate a suggested sleep technique into you and your baby's routine, don't hesitate to call on a real pro—talk to your pediatrician, and always prioritize safety over everything else.

Here's to sweet dreams for all!

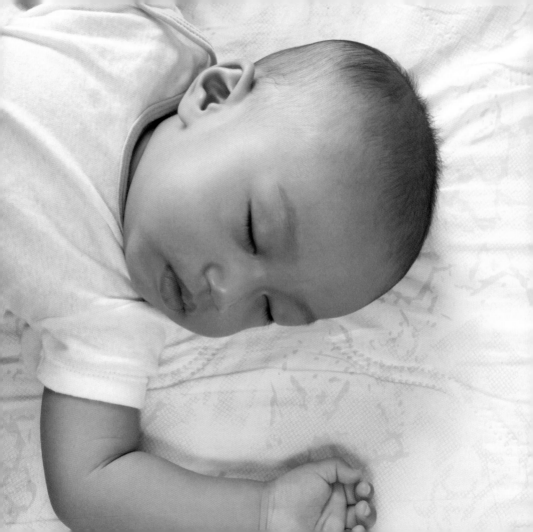

FOREWORD

And then they place your long-awaited baby into your loving arms.

You marvel at the delicacy of her features. You cry with joy when you inhale his skin, his breath. You are overcome with a sense of peace and excitement, happiness and connection to this small being. That first night is filled with your newborn's cries for food and comfort. You respond over and over again throughout the night and into the next day. Days turn into weeks and weeks turn into months of nighttime feedings as you adjust to continually interrupted sleep patterns. You are beyond tired. Way beyond tired. Sleep deprivation is real and oftentimes overwhelming, as there is a biological necessity to get your zzz's.

For some parents there is a natural rhythm of slumber and wake time, feeding and resting. It's a well-choreographed dance that just seems to work. But for the rest of us, it is an experience riddled with feelings of anxiety, frustration, and pure exhaustion. So how do you get a decent night's sleep? How do you navigate those times when you look at the clock, just after your baby has blissfully fallen back to sleep, and panic at the thought that you will be reawakened in a mere hour or two? Parents desperately search for answers in their quest for just a few more hours of rest to stave off their ever-present fatigue.

Simply stated, your baby's developing brain isn't wired for long periods of sleep. It is wired for attachment, stimulation, and nourishment. He needs to be held and fed often. She wants to feel your heartbeat and hear your voice. Newborns are learning how to handle being out of their cozy wombs where they were continually fed, rocked, and literally bombarded with sounds and sensations.

In order to grow and thrive, babies are programmed to be the center of your universe. So during these months, keep that in mind as you figure out just what your baby needs, wants, and loves. Whether it be a special song, your unique smell, swaddling, a dance that only you can do, the sounds of the wind rustling the trees, a pacifier, or an expensive teddy bear with recorded sounds of your heartbeat, only you can figure out what soothes your baby. That said, connecting with friends and gaining wisdom from family can enlighten you during these months. Remember to nurture yourself as well, so that you can, in turn, nurture your precious baby.

This book is full of wise suggestions and insights shared by parents, some of which are plain common sense and others delightfully innovative. Try some, dismiss others, and most importantly, create your own. It will give you solace to know that you are not alone and, yes, this sweet time (I promise that you'll think of it as such as the years fly by) will soon pass. Devour this book. You're awake anyway!

—Roni Cohen Leiderman, Ph.D.

NEWBORN BABY SLEEP MISTAKES

BY ALEXIS DUBIEF

① Mistake: Keeping Baby Awake Too Long

Most new parents are confused by how long their newborn baby should be awake because so many believe that they'll simply fall asleep when they need sleep (some will, most won't). Truthfully, most newborn babies can only stay awake about an hour. For the first few weeks your newborn baby may only be able to stay awake for thirty to forty minutes. Even if your baby *seems* content to stay awake for longer periods of time, it is in your and your baby's best interest to help her sleep more frequently. Overtired babies cry more and sleep poorly at night, so managing sleep throughout the day is a great way to make the first few months a happier time for everybody.

❷ Mistake: Keeping Baby Awake During the Day

Most newborns are surprisingly awake at night. Horrifyingly, this "playtime" often happens between 1:00 a.m. and 4:00 a.m., when no civilized parent has any interest in playing (and the TV selection is limited to infomercials and *Who's the Boss*). It is a commonly held myth that keeping baby awake during the day will solve this problem (this is the "tire them out so they sleep better" theory). This is patently untrue. Keeping baby awake during the day will simply make baby more tired and potentially exacerbate your night party problem. What will fix it?

Time.

When baby is up at night, keep the lights dim and activity to a minimum. No loud, blinky, bouncy toys. Most babies will organically sort out this day-night sleep reversal by about 6 weeks of age.

❸ Mistake: Trying to "Fix" Baby's Sleep

I love it when families take their children's sleep seriously. I really do. However, while there are many things about newborn sleep that parents may not love (awake at night, short naps, frequent feedings, etc.), part of being the parent of a newborn is accepting that for now, baby is driving the sleep bus.

Trying to force a schedule, getting frustrated with cat naps, feeling anxious about how much your baby sleeps, etc., are all losing strategies when you have a newborn. Which leads me to...

4 Mistake: Forcing the Crib

About 0 percent of newborn babies will sleep happily in a crib. I know you just spent $1,000 on that delightful Pottery Barn crib and can't wait to see your little peanut sleeping in it. But you and your peanut will be much happier and will get a lot more sleep if you accept that most babies aren't sleeping in the crib until sometime between 2 and 6 months of age (and sometimes later). For a newborn, the crib is huge and flat, which is pretty much the opposite of what they are used to. Where do they sleep? In co-sleepers, with Mom, in car seats, or my personal recommendation, in a swing.

Editor's Note: Allowing your baby to sleep in bed with you can be a serious safety risk. Always proceed with caution, as the risk of suffocation in your big cozy bed is a true concern for any little one. The American Academy of Pediatrics does not recommend sharing the same bed with your little one.

⑤ Mistake: Letting Baby Cry It Out

Listen tired peeps, there are definitely times and circumstances where crying it out (CIO) is the answer. This [newborn stage] is not one of those times.

⑥ Mistake: Worrying About Sleeping Through the Night

Your newborn baby might be sleeping through the night at 8 weeks. Or it may be 8 months. You may get a lucky night where she sleeps all night and then be horrified when it never happens again. I know how tired you are. For a year and a half, I would fantasize about leaving my baby home with my husband so I could go to a hotel and sleep blissfully uninterrupted for AS. LONG. AS. I. WANTED. Newborn sleep bounces around like an angry snake. You'll have hideous nights. Wonderful nights. And you'll never know what you're going to get. Don't worry about it. It won't be like this forever.

⑦ Mistake: Not Accepting Help

I see *many* couples that have convinced themselves that there is only one parent who has the skills to care for baby during the night. This is ridiculousness. If your partner can't care for baby at night then show them how. Put them through baby boot camp. Whatever you have to do to enable them to take some night parenting duties off your shoulders. If you're nursing and feel like it *has* to be you, start working on getting baby to take a bottle. (It doesn't get any easier as they get older so best to introduce this now.) Let Dad take one feeding a night while you get some uninterrupted sleep in the guest room. Don't allow yourself to be the sole baby zen master in the house.

8 Mistake: Not Using Sleep Aids

Parents will express their concerns about baby getting "addicted" or becoming dependent upon sleep aids (swaddling, pacifiers, swings, etc.). So their solution is to not use them and thus avoid sending their baby to White Noise Anonymous to deal with their sleep aid addiction. If your baby is under 6 months old, sleep aids are your friend. Embrace them. I promise you, your kid will be out of the swaddle by kindergarten.

9 Mistake: Not Sleeping When Baby Sleeps

After a few weeks you'll probably notice that there are general times of day when your baby is more likely to sleep in larger chunks. One of the first good chunks to develop is when they go to bed at night (generally after being awake for a longer period of time). So if you aren't going to bed when your baby does, you're missing out on the biggest window of uninterrupted sleep you're likely to get all day. I know the house is a mess, you haven't showered in a week, and the grass in your yard is so high that your neighbor's 5-year-old got lost in there. Forgetaboutit. Go to bed.

⑩ Mistake: Comparing Your Baby to THEIR Baby

In every new baby playgroup there is the blessed child who starts sleeping through the night at 4 weeks and takes huge chunky naps during the day. You will look at this well rested, recently showered parent and start to feel like you must have failed in some significant way. You haven't, they just got lucky. About 33 percent of babies are "easy"—they are easily soothed, fall asleep easily, sleep longer with less frequent night wakings, etc. It's just the way of the world. Your baby will get there too. Eventually.

—*ALEXIS DUBIEF is the author of www.preciouslittlesleep.com and* Precious Little Sleep

BEFORE BEDTIME

*Set Yourself Up
for Success with These
Pre-Bedtime Practices*

DAD TIP

"Let the kiddo nap. That's the biggest mistake I made with my first son—I thought I needed to let him get really tired if he was going to sleep well at night, but I learned quickly that an over-tired, cranky baby is much more challenging to lull to sleep than a baby fresh off of a normal naptime schedule."

—Dan, father of two

TEMP CHECK.

Don't overheat your baby! *You* may sleep best in a room that's warm and toasty, but babies actually sleep better in cooler temperatures, ideally hovering around 65 to 72 degrees Fahrenheit. And here's a bonus tip: Make sure he's dressed appropriately for the room temperature, and resist the urge to overdress him at night!

CRIB LOCATION.

Keep baby's crib away from windows, vents, or any other areas that may be drafty or conducive to sudden changes in temperature that could jar him awake.

GRANDMA TIP

"When the grandkids were little, I recorded myself reading each of them nursery rhymes and stories, even talking to them on the recording! Hearing their grandmother's voice seemed to put them all to sleep. Nowadays you buy stuffed animals and books to record your voice on, but I'm pleased with my 'old school' way."

—SYLVIA, GRANDMOTHER OF THREE

USE THE RIGHT FABRICS.

Your baby's skin is extremely sensitive so set yourself up for sleep success right off the bat by choosing the right fabrics for her pajamas, sheets, and blankets. Choose natural fibers to keep irritated skin at bay. Cotton is a favorite. And here's a bonus tip: Go with green-colored fabrics for some added serenity.

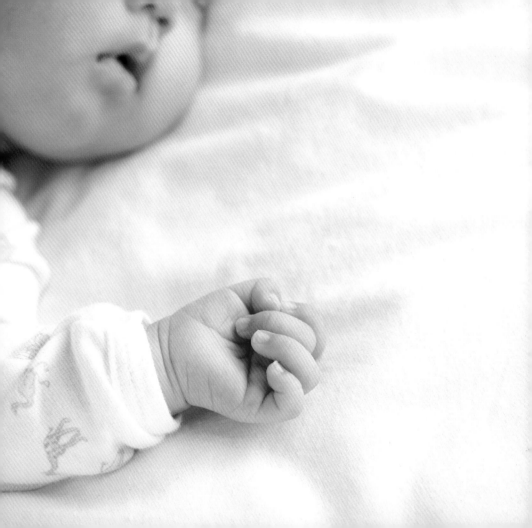

CLEAR THAT CRIB.

All a baby truly needs to sleep soundly is a good, firm mattress and a fitted sheet. Before putting baby into his crib, remove anything distracting or potentially dangerous— pillows, loose sheets and blankets, toys, plushes... it all should go.

MOM TIP

"To signal bedtime to my little guy, we have a sweet ritual of saying goodnight to the same people and things each night. We say 'goodnight' to his big brother, to the family dog, and to his most beloved stuffed animals. It helps settle him into the idea that it's bedtime."

—KELLY, MOTHER OF THREE

READ BABY'S BODY LANGUAGE.

Pay attention to how your baby signals his fatigue—it may not always be as obvious as a yawn! Keep an eye on your baby's pre-bed body language to properly respond to your sleepy baby's natural rhythms. If you let him get overtired, your sleep routine will be much more challenging.

SET A BEDTIME— AND STICK TO IT!

Help get your baby's circadian rhythm working in your favor! An ideal bedtime for your little one is between 7:00 p.m. and 8:00 p.m. Once you've established bedtime, do your best not to stray from it!

ESTABLISH A PRE-BEDTIME ROUTINE—AND TRY NOT TO WAVER FROM IT.

You'll find that it's easiest to lull your baby to sleep if you create a routine and do not stray from it. Babies benefit from consistency. And here's a second tip: Keep your sleep routine confined to your baby's bedroom, as moving from one space to another might jar your little one awake while you're trying to relax him.

MOM TIP

"When you establish your baby's sleep routine, do your best to create a ritual that you can recreate anywhere. This will allow you to travel with your kiddos and just be way more mobile and flexible—if you can stick to your sleep routine just as effectively at Grandma's as you can at home, you're golden."

—TRACIE, MOTHER OF FOUR

KEEP YOUR ROUTINE SHORT.

An overly involved and lengthy bedtime routine isn't sustainable— you will struggle to stick to it, and a longer pre-bedtime ritual won't necessarily lead to a better night's sleep than a shorter one. Try to find one or two tactics that work well for you and your baby, and keep it short!

MOM TIP

"My ultimate sleep tip has to be getting baby on a great schedule. I do the same thing every evening: I start with a healthy dinner, then a relaxing bath, a story, and bonding time. Typically, I rock both of my children and they just gradually fall asleep. I was able to start this (with both) at just a couple of weeks old. Now my babies are toddlers and we still follow this same routine. Our whole house is asleep by 8:00 p.m."

—BIANCA, MOTHER OF TWO

SIGNAL SLEEPTIME.

"You'll want to create special cues that signal bedtime sleep. A consistent, exact bedtime routine that begins at least thirty minutes before sleep time is very helpful in getting baby to organize his day/night sleep pattern."

—Elizabeth Pantley, *The No-Cry Sleep Solution*, 2002, McGraw-Hill Education, reprinted with permission from McGraw-Hill Education

LOSE THE NIGHTLIGHT.

Most babies sleep better in complete darkness, so resist the urge to install a nightlight, play with an iPad right before bed, or use dimmers in your baby's room—and even consider investing in blackout blinds to block out any light from outside, especially during a daytime nap!

DAD TIP

"My biggest piece of advice? Don't let your baby catch a second wind! If you've reached the tail end of your pre-bed ritual and something jars him awake, you'll have to start from the top, all over again. Protect your pre-bed baby time to keep interruptions at bay."

—JOSHUA, FATHER OF TWO

CALM DOWN WITH PRE-BED BATH TIME.

There's nothing more soothing than a hot bath after a long day—and your baby feels the same way! Join your precious one in a tub full of pure warm water (leave the soaps, salts, and bubble bath out of the equation), and let the experience relax you both, or let baby bathe solo with you by her side. And remember—don't fill the tub with toys that could risk having the opposite effect and stimulate him into an energized state.

BUY TWO OF EVERYTHING.

"There's this moment when I'm getting her ready for bed and I realize her puppy is nowhere to be found and oh, the scrambling. We've got a ton of back-up animals, and sometimes they work. Sometimes they don't. You know what I'm talking about, right? Except you're smarter than I am and have bought a few puppies in case one goes missing. That should be written on a form they give you when you leave the hospital with your baby: BUY TWO OF EVERYTHING, DUMMY."

—HEATHER B. ARMSTRONG, AUTHOR OF DOOCE.COM

AROMATHERAPY.

Babies are comforted by familiar smells. Find something in your room that carries your scent—perhaps a soft shirt that smells like Mom—and arrange the item near (but not in) the crib so he can fall asleep beside an aroma that he associates with you.

DECORATE WITH SERENE COLORS.

Don't be tempted to go overboard with bright and lively colors, like yellow, in your baby's room. Believe it or not, these colors can actually energize or even agitate your precious one! Instead, opt for cool green tones for your wallpaper or bedding, which are believed to have a calming effect on kiddos and adults alike.

PUTTING

BABY

TO SLEEP

*Foolproof Methods
of Lulling Your Baby
to Sleep at Night*

MASTER THE ART OF THE CRIB TRANSFER.

Don't undo all of the work you put into your bedtime routine by jarring your precious one awake when transferring him into his crib or bassinet! Try this method for a smooth and easy transition: Rather than having your arms under your baby (how will you pull them free once he's lowered into his crib?), hold your baby with your arms parallel to him, with his head still firmly supported by at least one of your hands. This way, you won't need to lurch your arms out from under him once he's settled into his crib and you can just lift them away without disturbing your baby.

THE
TICKLE MONSTER.

Australian father and YouTuber Nathan Dailo shared a video of lulling his baby to sleep by tickling the child's face with tissue paper oh-so-gently. Millions of views later, this method has proven successful for many sleepy parents!

DAD TIP

"I learned quickly to steer clear of extended eye contact when putting my baby to sleep. Whenever I locked eyes with my son, it seemed to immediately capture his interest and rouse him, undoing all of the work I put into our calming pre-bed ritual."

—ASHISH, FATHER OF TWO

READ A BEDTIME STORY.

But not just any story. Choose a book with a consistent, calming rhythm, ideally one that rhymes. The hypnotic, repetitive cadence of your voice will help put your baby to sleep. And here's an additional tip: Read a real, physical book, not a story on your iPad. The backlit screen will not help calm your baby before bed.

SING A LULLABY.

There's a reason this is the oldest trick in the book. Whether you're cooing over his crib or rocking him in your arms while you sing, a melodic lullaby sung in dulcet tones is a classic go-to method for lulling a baby to sleep—literally! Choose a song with a repetitive rhythm and a consistent range to avoid jarring shifts in volume or pitch that could jolt your baby awake. Sing or hum softly, and repeat the same song on a loop until your baby drifts off.

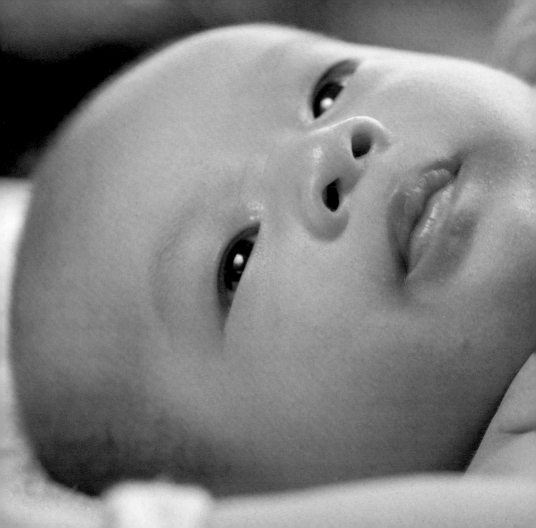

MOM TIP

"Forget about classic lullabies—
my sons would drift off to my
husband's rendition of James
Taylor's hit 'Sweet Baby James.'
It was a surprising lifesaver when
I had three fussy little ones!"

—CHRISTIN, MOTHER OF THREE

CONDITION A RESPONSE.

"You can induce sleep by giving your child a warm bath, reading him a story, and even adopting a simple gesture like stroking a finger from the forehead down to the top of the nose. Some kids get so good at this conditioned response that it takes only two or three strokes before their eyes start getting heavy."

—MICHAEL F. ROIZEN, M.D. AND MEHMET C. OZ, M.D., *YOU RAISING YOUR CHILD*

PLAY
CLASSICAL MUSIC.

The gentle orchestral tones of classical music can lull a baby into sleep mode in the same way that it helps you unwind after a long day. Put a classical music playlist or CD on a loop for continual play, or let the music reach a stopping point once your baby has drifted off. Avoid music streaming services like Pandora that interrupt music with advertisements—the last thing you need is an obnoxious voiceover jarring your little guy awake!

CHAT WITH BABY.

Why not help your munchkin unwind the same way that you and your partner close out the evening: by chatting about your day! Speak calmly and softly into your baby's ear—try to avoid baby talk, if you can—describing the events of your day. As you loosen up and settle into your evening, your baby will, too!

MOM TIP

"Two tips that I learned from my youngest son: Ryan loved it when I would put my head on his when he was lying down. It would put him to sleep in less than five minutes...seriously! Also, I learned that Ryan actually benefitted from our boisterously noisy household when it came time to go to sleep. He was never habituated to complete silence or white noise, so he adjusted to a fairly noisy environment and learned to sleep through any noise level in the house, including the vacuum."

—CHRIS, MOTHER OF THREE

SKIN-TO-SKIN SOOTHING.

Babies find comfort in close proximity to their parents, and there's no closer contact than skin-on-skin. Lie on your back and rest your baby on your stomach, belly-down. Remove your baby's shirt and roll up your own top so that you're resting together belly-to-belly, skin-to-skin. Breathe deeply and stroke his back while he drifts off to sleep.

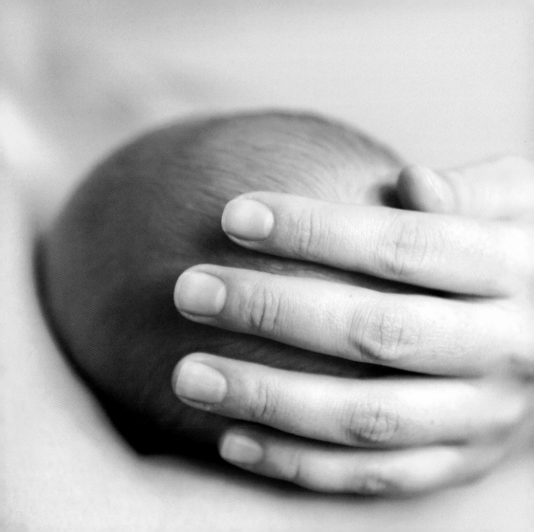

HEAD RUB.

You can probably put your partner to sleep with a good head rub, so why not your little one? Stroke her head softly with your fingertips while she's resting in her crib or bassinet. Make very gentle circular motions with your fingers to lull your baby to sleep with a soothing, therapeutic head rub.

TRY CO-SLEEPING.

If your baby isn't ready for a crib, try a co-sleeper. Place one next to your own bed and you can both grab some zzzz's! The American Academy of Pediatrics advises against bringing your infant into your own bed with you as it presents a wide range of safety concerns, but having your precious one close by in a co-sleeper can be just as comforting to you both.

"Birthing balls aren't just
for birthing—I used to bounce
on mine with my newborn in my
lap. The gentle up-and-down
motion would always
lull her to sleep."

—Brittany, mother of one

DANCE WITH YOUR BABY.

If your baby is lulled by gentle, repetitive motion, take rocking to the next level and give a "baby dance" a try. Cradle your baby closely against your body and sway back and forth as you stand upright. Move in a rhythmic, predictable motion to help your baby drift off.

INDOOR WATERFALL.

If your bathroom—or the kitchen sink—is within earshot of your baby's crib, bassinet, or co-sleeper, try turning on the shower or faucet as an unconventional approach to white noise (or, draw yourself a bath so that the water doesn't go to waste!). The sound of running water is very soothing to adults and babies alike, and you likely won't have to let that water run for long before your baby drifts off to the hypnotic rhythms of running water.

THE "COLIC HOLD."

Position your little one so
he's on your forearm, belly-down.
Make sure his head and neck are
fully supported by your hand.
Hold him firmly and securely,
tight against your body, and gently
rock and sway, back and forth, as
he falls asleep. Your baby needn't
have colic for this to work.

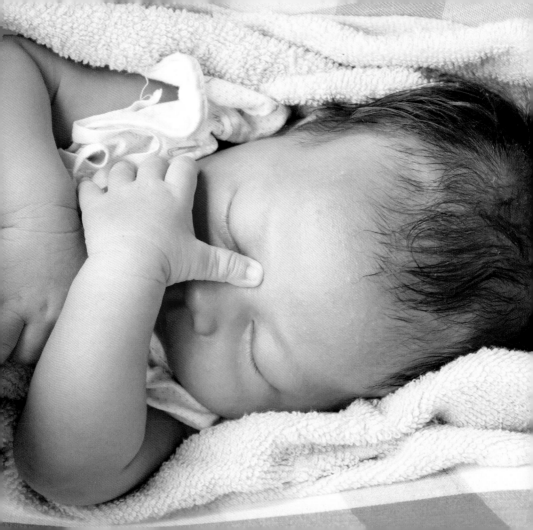

MOM TIP

"I Ferberized (from Richard Ferber, a doctor in pediatric sleep disorders) my daughter when she was about three months old. After putting her in her crib awake, I would wait for gradually longer amounts of time after she started crying before comforting her. She learned to self-soothe and also learned to fall asleep on her own. Best thing I ever did!"

—BONNIE, MOTHER OF TWO

LET YOUR BABY FALL BACK TO SLEEP—WITHOUT INTERFERING.

"Put your child into the crib or bed awake, in the place you want him to be sleeping for the night. Let him fall asleep under the same circumstances that will be present when he wakes normally during the night (in his crib or bed, not being held or rocked). Let him fall back asleep the same way after nighttime wakings. If he cries or calls for you at bedtime or upon waking at night, check him briefly at increasing intervals...Any schedule will work, as long as the waiting periods increase progressively, and as long as you continue the process long enough for your child to get practice falling asleep under the desired conditions."

—RICHARD FERBER, M.D.,
SOLVE YOUR CHILD'S SLEEP PROBLEMS

SOOTHE A
FUSSY
BABY

*Sleep Solutions for Nights
When Baby Is Sick, Teething,
or Just Plain Fussy*

FUSSY FOR A REASON?

Before you try any other method in this section, do a quick state-of-the-union: check for signs of ear infections, fever, or any other physical ailment that might be causing your little one's fussiness. If you think there are extenuating circumstances, be sure to talk to your pediatrician immediately.

COULD IT BE A FOOD SENSITIVITY?

If you notice that your baby is experiencing discomfort after his bedtime meal and it's keeping him from falling asleep, consider the possibility of a food allergy or sensitivity (like dairy or gluten), or a gastrointestinal or gastroesophageal issue. Talk to your pediatrician if this might be what's keeping your fussy baby awake.

SWADDLE.

While swaddling as a way to help with calming and sleeping has been around for a long time, recent studies warn against this method without using proper technique. Talk to your pediatrician about her recommendations for the ideal swaddling technique, and if you have any doubts about your ability to properly and safely swaddle your little one, please exercise caution and forgo this method. You can also try a **Sleep Sack** for a similar effect.

But be warned: one of the major concerns in regards to swaddling is hip dysplasia. The International Hip Dysplasia Institute recommends against swaddling the legs extended and pressed tightly together. Instead the hips should have room to move and legs should be able to bend up and out. After swaddling, don't lay your baby face down, but rather lay him on his back, face up. Stop routinely swaddling when your baby is actively trying to roll over.

TAKE A DEEP BREATH.

"The effect of deep breathing helps slow both your own heart rate and your child's heart rate, which allows the body to relax and slow down. You can literally feel your heart rate slow down, your mind get quieter, and your whole body physically relax. You can literally feel your child's heart rate slow down, as they start to relax and melt right into you. This is why I always do the deep breathing in a hugging position. It washes over you and your child like a calming, relaxing sleepytime medicine."

—Lauren Tamm, www.themilitarywifeandmom.com

GET ZEN.

Your baby can sense if you're anxious. And chances are, if your little one is being exceptionally fussy, you're getting frustrated. If deep breathing isn't enough, try chanting a soothing mantra. Close your eyes, and quietly chant a short, calming phrase to yourself, over and over again. The repetitive chanting may even help your fussy little one get zen!

TRUST YOUR INSTINCTS.

"First-time parents may have more trouble with this one, but eventually, you will get the hang of it. If you feel like something is off, don't worry about whether or not you're being paranoid. Go check. And if you have to go pee in the cat's litter box, because you're terrified that the sounds of rustling around in the bathroom might wake the baby, well, there's a lot to be said for paranoid when it comes to sleeping babies! If they're not sleeping well, then you're not sleeping well. So do what you have to do. We won't judge."

—Love Barnett, www.scarymommy.com

FOREHEAD STROKE.

A light, soft stroke to your baby's face, especially the bridge of his nose or his forehead, can produce surprisingly calming effects and help lull him to sleep.

GENTLE EYE STROKE.

Try stroking your baby
very gently around her eyes
with a feather-light touch
to soothe and calm her.

MOM TIP

"My daughter was a colicky baby, and for whatever reason, she was lulled to sleep by the sound of our vacuum cleaner. As you can imagine, the apartment stayed very clean after I discovered that secret trick! When she was older and outgrew the colic, she loved it when I rocked her and caressed her face, especially her eyebrows and the bridge of her nose."

—JASMIN, MOTHER OF ONE

SHOULDER HUG.

A tried-and-true position that facilitates a baby's relaxation is holding her up against your shoulder. This upright position allows for the type of diaphragmatic breathing that can alleviate tummy pressure and discomfort, and help her fall asleep. You may even get a nice big burp out of her.

GO FOR A DRIVE.

A ride in the car is the classic way to help babies fall asleep—whether you want them to or not! A car seat with a detachable base that stays in the car makes it easy to transport your baby from car to house seamlessly, without waking the little tyke up! Just be sure to do your research to find the safest model out there.

MOM TIP

"My baby always drifts off in the stroller when we're out for walks during the day. It's inconvenient to take her outside in the stroller at night when we're winding down for the evening, so I've taken to pushing her around our hallways inside in the stroller before bedtime— it works like a charm!"

—COLLEEN, MOTHER OF ONE

SURPRISE!

If your baby is in the throes of an especially challenging tantrum, an unexpected noise or sensation may surprise him out of his distress. Perhaps flip on your fan and let the sudden sensation of wind on his face distract him from his weep-fest!

SWITCH THINGS UP.

Sometimes all it takes is a new voice, a new set of hands, or a new rocking rhythm to set your baby on the path to snoozeville. If you've been rocking or singing without success, try handing her off to your partner, or even a big sibling (if he or she is old enough!), to switch up your routine when your baby is especially fussy. It could make all the difference!

FOOT MASSAGE.

As long as your baby's feet aren't especially ticklish, gently massaging your baby's feet, one at a time, is a great way to calm him down. Take his little foot in both hands and apply pressure softly, moving your fingers and thumbs in slow, circular motions for a smooth, consistent foot massage.

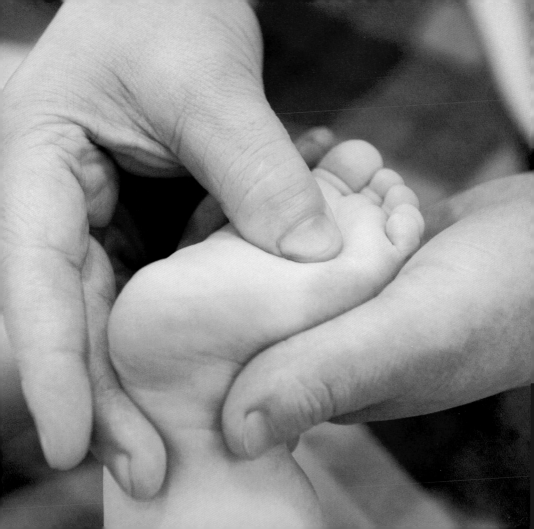

MOM TIP

"I learned early on that my fussy baby could always be calmed down by something exciting or distracting to focus on. Not a glowing, backlit TV screen, but something just naturally engaging like our fish tank or hamster cage. Watching our fish slowly mill around in their tank or our hamster rhythmically run on its wheel never failed to leave her feeling soothed, happy, and ready for her bedtime routine."

—YAEL, MOTHER OF ONE

AWAKE AGAIN?

*Lull Your Baby **Back** to Sleep When Little One Starts Stirring*

GOT MILK?

No one can sleep when they're hungry—maybe baby just needs some nourishment. This is the most common reason that a baby will wake up in the middle of the night. (I mean, I wake up hungry sometimes, too! Who doesn't love a midnight snack?)

BREAST OR BOTTLE.

"One of the surprises of parenting that may fall in the category of 'no one ever told me' is that breast-fed babies typically sleep for shorter periods and are usually older when they finally begin to sleep through the night. Why do breast-fed babies sleep for shorter periods? Since breast milk is much easier for babies to digest than formula, it means shorter intervals between feedings.

So a baby at 8 weeks
may still be breast-feeding every
two or three hours throughout the
night, while a bottle-fed baby may be
sleeping for up to four to six hours a
night. These trends don't hold for all
babies, of course. Your baby may do
the exact opposite. But as a whole,
these are the likely effects of breast-
feeding and bottle-feeding on your
baby's sleeping pattern."

—JODI A. MINDELL, PH.D.,
SLEEPING THROUGH THE NIGHT

DREAMFEED.

Made popular by *The Baby Whisperer*, this method will actually help you avoid nighttime wakings due to hunger. Rather than letting hunger pangs rouse your little one awake, be pro-active: calmly and quietly give your drowsy child an additional feeding prior to *your* own bedtime.

"By the time my daughter was a couple months old, she didn't like to have to cry to signal that she needed something, so she hated to be away from me in her crib—until she discovered the noise-making toy attached to the end of her crib. All she had to do was kick it and she'd make so much ruckus that we'd know she was up and would go get her—before the crying started. And, as a result, she didn't mind being put down in her crib, as long as she was close enough to be able to kick the noisemakers. Many years later, long after she'd forgotten about the kick-toy, she said she wondered why she'd always kick when she first woke up, which is why her cat would sleep by her head instead of by her feet."

—AMY, MOTHER OF ONE

COUNT BACKWARDS FROM 100.

You've heard that counting backwards is a good technique to calm your own mind when sleep isn't coming, so why not try it on your little one? Lay your baby on her back in her crib or co-sleeper, and gently stroke up and down her arms and across her forehead while you softly coo the numbers backwards, at a slow but consistent clip. Baby will likely doze off before you hit 50!

KEEP THE ROOM DARK.

When your baby wakes up in the middle of the night, resist the urge to flick on the light switch when attending to him. Keep the room dark, and gently rock him back and forth until he starts to doze again. Put him back in his crib as he's drifting off so that he can settle himself and return to sleep.

STAY CLOSE.

"When the baby is in the crib, reassure him that although you are not going to pick him up, you are right there. Stand next to the crib, or sit on a glider ottoman or chair so you are close to the baby."

— SUZY GIORDANO AND LISA ABIDIN, *THE BABY SLEEP SOLUTION: A PROVEN PROGRAM TO TEACH YOUR BABY TO SLEEP TWELVE HOURS A NIGHT*

MOM TIP

"Your baby monitor is your best friend. The middle-of-the-night-wake-up is a delicate balancing act. If you jump at each sound you hear from the crib, chances are you'll just disrupt your baby's sleep. But then, if you wait until your baby is fully awake, it's so much harder to get her back to sleep. I quickly learned which noises signaled that

she was starting to stir for real.
When I would hear those telltale
sounds through the monitor,
I would creep into her room and
give a gentle belly rub or face rub
to soothe her back to sleep while
she was still in that 'sweet spot'
before being fully roused awake—
it really helped a lot."

—MANDY, MOTHER OF FOUR

CREATE YOUR OWN WHITE NOISE.

If your baby doesn't sleep with white noise, creating your own calming sound effects in your baby's ear can be the perfect way to lull him back to sleep. Try mimicking ocean waves by softly making "shhhh" sounds with your lips close to his ears. Another benefit of a "shhhh" sound effect? Some experts say that it closely resembles the sound of your blood flow, which he spent nine months listening to in the comfort of your womb!

TEACH SELF-SOOTHING.

This method takes time, and there are so many ways to instill self-soothing habits in your little one—entire books have been written on the subject. The most effective way to begin teaching your little one to self-soothe in times of fussiness is to gradually substitute vocal soothing in place of physical soothing. In other words, if your baby is used to being held when she's getting fussy, try replacing that method with reassuring coos to calm her down. This is a solid first step toward helping your baby soothe herself.

MOM TIP

"Don't. Freak. Out. I was an extremely nervous new mom. Whenever I thought I detected the slightest rustling sound through the baby monitor, I would leap out of bed and go check on my first-born. Usually, the poor guy was just shifting in his sleep, but my bursting in never failed to wake him up for real. I should have just let him be!"

—TAMEKA, MOTHER OF TWO

GAS BE GONE.

Sometimes a sleepless baby
is fussy for the simplest reason: gas.
Try this unusual method of relieving
your precious one of uncomfortable
gas and pressure: gently take one
little leg in each hand, and move
them in a rotating motion,
simulating the leg movement
of riding a bicycle.

THE FAKE OUT.

If your baby is soothed by breastfeeding but you know that Junior isn't especially hungry, try the "Fake Out" method: Take him in your arms and position him against your breast as if you're going to nurse him. As he relaxes against you to get ready for this calming and familiar routine, pop a pacifier into his mouth, instead of your nipple! Lower him back into his crib or cradle and let him self-soothe until sleep comes.

MOM TIP

"Neither one of you will sleep if you just let her wail, especially when she's brand new. So trust your instincts and do what comes naturally when she's *really* shrieking: respond to her cries. And here's a bonus tip, which is of chief importance: Sleep when she sleeps. You have to."

—OLIVIA, MOTHER OF TWO

TOOLS
OF THE
TRADE

Our Top Picks for Tools, Furniture,
Gadgets, and Apps Engineered
to Lull Your Baby to Sleep

BABY SWING.

Movement, such as swaying, bouncing, or rocking, can easily calm a restless baby. Baby swings cradle and gently move your baby, and nowadays many come with mobile device connectivity and 180 degrees of motion. Graco, Ingenuity, and 4moms are among the top brands for these swings.

THE DRYER.

If your baby is soothed by the gentle rocking and rumbling of a car ride but you don't have time to take your little one out for a drive, try creating the same experience atop your dryer! Secure your child carefully into her car seat or a baby seat (with you next to her, holding on tight), flip on the dryer, and let the gentle vibrating motion lull her to sleep.

HIKING BACKPACK OR BABY CARRIER.

If you love staying active, don't let
a restless baby get in the way of your
exercise routines. Secure your little one
into a baby backpack or carrier and
take an evening stroll. Ideally, keep the
rhythm of your steps consistent.
The gentle bouncing motion will
lull your baby right to sleep.

SLING.

When you're out and about, keep Junior close in a baby sling, where he will be lulled to sleep by the motion and being close to his parent. There are quite a few versions available, and can make fashionable additions to your outfit; they can even look like scarves! Try the Baby K'tan or Moby Wrap carriers.

MOM TIP

"Don't be afraid to call in favors! You know those single or childless friends who are miffed that you can't meet them for drinks late at night like you used to? They'll understand the demands of your new life if you invite them to stay for the weekend and put them to work.

Let someone who's recently slept for more than two hours straight take over some of the rocking duty. And what about your mother-in-law? You know she's dying to help anyway—might as well direct her energy in a way that will help you out!"

—BINDI, MOTHER OF THREE

ROCKING CHAIR.

This nursery classic is an old favorite of parents and grandparents alike, and for good reason! Rocking and swaying motions top the list of ways to soothe your baby to sleep, and these chairs don't have to be the standard wooden version. Modern versions can look like a regular armchair, and may glide or recline too!

OVERNIGHT DIAPERS.

If you notice that a nighttime bathroom habit seems to consistently jar your baby awake, it might be time to call in the big guns: seek out extra absorbent diapers that are specifically engineered for overnight use. Don't make a habit of this and make sure you use plenty of diaper rash ointment to protect your little one's skin, but it could fend off the middle-of-the-night diaper changes that prevent a solid night's sleep.

PACIFIER (OR FINGER!).

Let your baby self-soothe with this classic go-to—or his own fingers. You can even store them in a pacifier holder so they don't get dirty. According to WebMD, pacifiers have additional benefits for babies, like helping prevent SIDS and satisfying his "suck reflex."

"Before Olivia was born, our dog Simon was the baby of the house...with a very loud mouth. People kept saying, 'Enjoy your sleep now, because you'll never sleep again with an infant!' Ha! If they only knew about Simon's nighttime barking habits. I can't stress enough how piercing his little barks can be. When I was pregnant, Olivia would actually react to the sound of his barking. If she can hear him while floating around in my belly, I thought, he'll inevitably wake her when she's here snoozing in a cradle next to the bed. Fast-forward to our first night home with little Olivia: the dread immediately set in.

My husband and I waking up, terrified that she wasn't breathing or she would find a way to fly out of the cradle. She was, of course, totally fine and actually slept quite peacefully. In fact, every time she made a sound, Simon would jolt up and bark at us to check up on her. The amazing thing is, every time he yipped or barked, she settled down and went back to sleep. After nine months of hearing him barking while she was in utero, the noise actually comforted her. Who needs those fancy sleep sound machines or a nighttime nanny when you have a yappy little papillon!"

—Jaime, mother of one

WHITE NOISE DEVICES.

White noise is super soothing for babies! Plus it can drown out the unpredictable household sounds that are at risk of jarring your little one awake. Here are five different options, each offering a different type of sound or experience—all are among the most highly recommended devices available:

★ Graco Sweet Slumber Sound Machine

★ Cloud B Soothing Sounds Plush (pick a favorite stuffed animal, like a lamb or giraffe!)

★ Skip Hop Moonlight & Melodies Nightlight Soother

★ Dohm for Baby White Noise Sound Machine

★ myBaby HoMedics SoundSpa On-The-Go

WHITE NOISE APPS TO THE RESCUE.

You may not have room in the budget for a fancy white noise device, but not to worry. Some truly awesome white noise apps are at your fingertips, ready to download straight to your smart phone or tablet (many of them at no cost!). Each offers up a different way to lull your baby:

★ **Relax Melodies: Sleep Zen Sounds and White Noise for Meditation, Yoga, and Baby Relaxation by iLBSoft (Free)**

★ **Sleep Pillow Sounds by Fitness22 LTD (Free)**

★ **Sound Sleeper by Michael Feigenson (Free)**

★ **Deep Calm by Imagination Unlimited (Free)**

★ **Lullaby Baby by Lost Ego Studios Limited ($0.99)**

AWESOME APPS FOR SLEEPTIME.

The world of apps created just for parents and their new babies is full of inventive sleep aids. We've tested out dozens and zeroed in on our five favorites, each of which provides a unique way to lull your little one:

★ **Johnson's Bedtime Baby Sleep App by Johnson & Johnson Consumer Companies, Inc. (Free)**

★ **Baby Music Pro by Meditation Sleep Center (Free)**

★ **Sprout Baby Tracker by Med ART Studios (Free or $2.99 and up for more features)**

★ **Shwssh – The Baby Sleep Aid by SilverTree Technology ($0.99)**

★ **Baby Sleep Training Guide by WhaleParadise Labs ($2.99)**

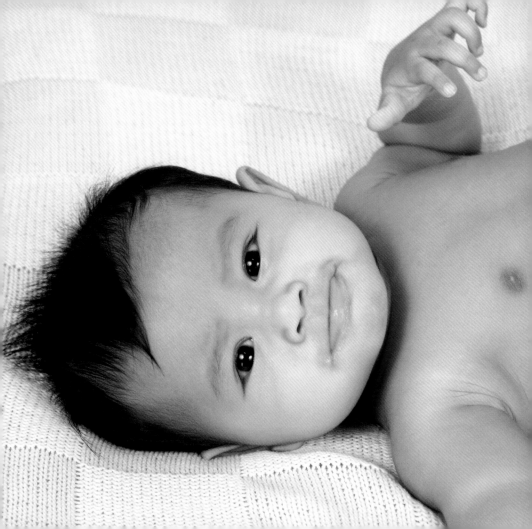

VIDEO BABY MONITOR.

Although they can range in cost from $50 to $300 or more, the investment is worth it if your baby sleeps in a crib or in a separate room. The ability to see your baby as he drifts in and out of sleep is vital if you're prone to responding to every little sound that you hear coming from his room, which may end up startling him awake. A video monitor will help you pick and choose when your baby truly needs you, and when you can let him self-soothe.

SPIRE.

We've talked about "getting zen" and taking deep breaths—now you can let an app remind you of this, too! This device is for you, not your baby, but it will be a huge help to you both. Spire is a cool device that syncs up to a smart phone app. Wear it on your bra strap or waist band to monitor your heart rate and breathing; it will buzz you when you're getting stressed or tense. Respond to these buzzes with deep, calming breaths—as you relax, your baby will, too.

SLEEP SACK.

A "wearable blanket" for babies, this useful tool is a great alternative to a loose blanket (which could risk causing suffocation). The HALO brand is sleeveless, ensuring that baby won't overheat, and HALO also promotes its "roomy sack design," which reduces the risk of hip dysplasia. Slip the sack over his usual PJs for a safe and cozy slumber!

PARENT TIP

"Our little baby has a special, cozy sleeper that's only for night night! We never dress him in it during the day to help him understand the difference between day and night, based on our sartorial choices. Once we settle into a nice dark room, we feed him and sing a bit, and then rock him gently in our arms until he falls asleep."

—Sam and Elana, parents of one

ESSENTIAL OILS.

These aromatic and soothing oils go a long way in helping adults relax, so why not babies, too? Pediatricians strongly advise against ever using an essential oil directly on your baby's skin, even if it's diluted in a carrier oil, but there are other ways that you can use essential oils. First, always be sure to carefully read the oil's label, or check with your own pediatrician, to ensure that it's recommended for babies—remember, not all oils are created equal. Here are two great ways to help lull your baby to sleep using essential oils:

★ Place a drop of an essential oil like lavender or chamomile on a washcloth near (but not in!) a baby's crib to help to relax your little one. These scents are known to calm and soothe harried adults and fussy babies alike. Try this technique for babies who are older than six months old.

★ Invest in a high-quality diffuser. About half an hour prior to tucking your baby in at night, diffuse a lavender oil in your baby's room. Again, only use this method if your little one is at least six months old.

LEARN WHAT MAKES YOUR BABY SPECIAL.

It doesn't need to be said: every baby is different, unique, special. Every baby will respond differently to the wide range of tools, tactics and routines we've suggested. Some babies are entranced by twinkling Christmas lights in a way that calms them before bedtime, while others are jarred wide awake by the little blinking bulbs. Maybe your baby loves the sound of the piano, or maybe she relishes skin-to-skin contact with Dad to soothe her before bedtime. Practice makes perfect—try out as many "ways" in this book as you can, and see what makes your baby tick! You'll establish the perfect bedtime ritual in no time.

A FINAL NOTE: DON'T BE AFRAID TO EXPERIMENT!

As your baby gets older, chances are he might outgrow the methods that worked when he was a newborn. If your usual routine stops having the impact it once did, change it up! Adjust your baby's bedtime, replace your typical lullaby with some Bach, or introduce a new type of white noise into the mix.

INDEX

ABOUT THE FOREWORD WRITER

Roni Cohen Leiderman, Ph.D., is an educator, author, and consultant in the fields of child development, family relationships, parenting, and autism and currently serves as the dean of Nova Southeastern University's Mailman Segal Center for Human Development. She is the author of numerous books including *Let's Play Together: Playful Parenting Games and Activities for Nurturing Your Child's Development, Baby Play, 365 Activities You and Your Toddler Will Love*, and *Play and Learn: 1001 Fun Activities for Your Baby and Child*. Dr. Leiderman contributes to parenting columns, appears on television, Internet, and radio programming, and contributes to national periodicals and publications.

ABOUT THE AUTHOR

Alexandra Paige is a passionate reader, writer, and researcher who interviewed dozens of moms, dads, brothers, sisters, friends, family, grandparents, aunts, and uncles to discover the most reliable, foolproof—and just plain creative—ways to lull a baby to sleep for this book.

ABOUT CIDER MILL PRESS

Good ideas ripen with time. From seed to harvest,
Cider Mill Press brings fine reading, information, and entertainment
together between the covers of its creatively crafted books.
Our Cider Mill bears fruit twice a year, publishing
a new crop of titles each spring and fall.

"Where Good Books Are Ready for Press"
Visit us on the Web at
www.cidermillpress.com
or write to us at
PO Box 454
Kennebunkport, Maine 04046